Berwyn Public Library
2701 Harlem Ave.
Berwyn, IL 60402

W9-CFB-598
3 2957 00259 9408

DISCARD

Berwyn Public Library
2701 Harlem Ave.
Berwyn, IL 60402

BERWYN PUBLIC LIBRARY

ANIMALS ANIMALES
THAT LIVE ON THE QUE VIVEN EN LA
FARM GRANJA

Chickens/
Las gallinas

JoAnn Early Macken

Reading consultant/Consultora de lectura:
Susan Nations, M.Ed.,
author/literacy coach/consultant

WEEKLY WR READER®
EARLY LEARNING LIBRARY

Please visit our web site at: www.earlyliteracy.cc
For a free color catalog describing Weekly Reader® Early Learning Library's list of high-quality books, call 1-877-445-5824 (USA) or 1-800-387-3178 (Canada). Weekly Reader® Early Learning Library's fax: (414) 336-0164.

Library of Congress Cataloging-in-Publication Data available upon request from publisher. Fax (414) 336-0157 for the attention of the Publishing Records Department.

ISBN 0-8368-4285-5 (lib. bdg.)
ISBN 0-8368-4292-8 (softcover)

This edition first published in 2005 by
Weekly Reader® Early Learning Library
330 West Olive Street, Suite 100
Milwaukee, WI 53212 USA

Copyright © 2005 by Weekly Reader® Early Learning Library

Picture research: Diane Laska-Swanke
Art direction: Tammy West
Cover design and page layout: Kami Koenig
Translators: Colleen Coffey and Consuelo Carrillo

Photo credits: Cover, pp. 7, 11, 13, 15, 17, 19, 21 Gregg Andersen;
p. 5 © James P. Rowan; p. 9 © Norvia Behling

All rights reserved. No part of this book may be reproduced, stored in a retrieval system, or transmitted in any form or by any means, electronic, mechanical, photocopying, recording, or otherwise, without the prior written permission of the copyright holder.

Printed in the United States of America

1 2 3 4 5 6 7 8 9 08 07 06 05 04

Note to Educators and Parents

Reading is such an exciting adventure for young children! They are beginning to integrate their oral language skills with written language. To encourage children along the path to early literacy, books must be colorful, engaging, and interesting; they should invite the young reader to explore both the print and the pictures.

Animals That Live on the Farm is a new series designed to help children read about the behavior and life cycles of farm animals. Each book describes a different type of animal and explains why and how it is raised.

Each book is specially designed to support the young reader in the reading process. The familiar topics are appealing to young children and invite them to read — and re-read — again and again. The full-color photographs and enhanced text further support the student during the reading process.

In addition to serving as wonderful picture books in schools, libraries, homes, and other places where children learn to love reading, these books are specifically intended to be read within an instructional guided reading group. This small group setting allows beginning readers to work with a fluent adult model as they make meaning from the text. After children develop fluency with the text and content, the book can be read independently. Children and adults alike will find these books supportive, engaging, and fun!

Una nota a los educadores y a los padres

¡La lectura es una emocionante aventura para los niños! En esta etapa están comenzando a integrar su manejo del lenguaje oral con el lenguaje escrito. Para fomentar la lectura desde una temprana edad, los libros deben ser vistosos, atractivos e interesantes; deben invitar al joven lector a explorar tanto el texto como las ilustraciones.

Animales que viven en la granja es una nueva serie pensada para ayudar a los niños a conocer la conducta y los ciclos de vida de los animales de la granja. Cada libro describe un tipo diferente de animal y explica por qué y cómo se cria.

Cada libro ha sido especialmente diseñado para facilitar el proceso de lectura. La familiaridad con los temas tratados atrae la atención de los niños y los invita a leer — y releer — una y otra vez. Las fotografías a todo color y el tipo de letra facilitan aún más al estudiante el proceso de lectura.

Además de servir como fantásticos libros ilustrados en la escuela, la biblioteca, el hogar y otros lugares donde los niños aprenden a amar la lectura, estos libros han sido concebidos específicamente para ser leídos en grupos de instrucción guiada. Este contexto de grupos pequeños permite que los niños que se inician en la lectura trabajen con un adulto cuya fluidez les sirve de modelo para comprender el texto. Una vez que se han familiarizado con el texto y el contenido, los niños pueden leer los libros por su cuenta. ¡Tanto niños como adultos encontrarán que estos libros son útiles, entretenidos y divertidos!

— Susan Nations, M.Ed., author, literacy coach,
and consultant in literacy development

Peep! Peep! A **chick** hatches out of an egg. A chick is a baby chicken.

- - - - - - - -

¡Pío, pío! El **pollito** sale del cascarón de un huevo. El pollito es un pollo recién nacido.

Chicks have fluffy yellow feathers. A chick's feathers are called **down**.

- - - - - - -

Los pollitos tienen las plumas esponjadas y amarillas. El plumaje del pollito se llama **plumón**.

A grown female chicken is a **hen**.   A grown male chicken is a **rooster**.

- - - - - - -

La hembra adulta es la **gallina**. El macho adulto es el **gallo**.

Chickens peck at food.
They scratch at shiny
things on the ground.

– – – – – – –

Las gallinas picotean la
comida. Escarban las cosas
brillantes de la tierra.

Chickens eat seeds, plants, fruit, and berries. They also eat insects and worms.

- - - - - - -

Las gallinas comen semillas, plantas, fruta y granos. Comen insectos y lombrices también.

To drink, a chicken takes a sip of water. It tilts its head back. The water runs down its throat.

— — — — — — —

Para beber, la gallina toma un sorbo de agua. Mueve la cabeza hacia atrás. El agua baja por la garganta.

Chickens clean their feathers with their beaks. Chickens take dust baths to get rid of insect pests.

- - - - - - - -

Las gallinas se limpian las plumas con el pico. Las gallinas se bañan en tierra para quitarse los insectos molestos.

Chickens stay in small groups. At night, the chickens stay inside a coop. There, the chickens are safe from predators.

Las gallinas se quedan en pequeños grupos. Por la noche, las gallinas se queden en el gallinero. Allí las gallinas están protegidas de los depredadores.

19

Farmers keep chickens for meat and eggs. Have you ever seen chickens on a farm?

- - - - - - -

Los granjeros crían las gallinas para carne y huevos. ¿Alguna vez has visto gallinas en una granja?

Glossary/Glosario

coop — a small building where chickens are kept

gallinero — una pequeña construcción donde se guardan las gallinas

hatches — comes out of an egg

sale del cascarón de un huevo — sale de un huevo

peck — to strike or pick up with the bill

picotear — golpear o recoger con el pico

predators — animals that eat other animals

depredadores — animales que se comen los otros animales

For More Information/Más información

Books/Libros

Chickens. Farm Animals (series). Rachael Bell (Heinemann)

Chickens on the Farm. On the Farm (series). Mari C. Schuh (Pebble Books)

Chicks & Chickens. Gail Gibbons (Holiday House)

From Chick to Chicken. Jillian Powell (Raintree/Steck Vaughn)

Web Sites/Páginas Web

Life on a Chicken Farm
www.mda.state.mi.us/kids/stories/farmlife/chickens/
Taking care of chickens

Index/Índice

chicks/pollitos 4, 6
cleaning/limpiarse 16
coops/gallineros 18
down/plumón 6
drinking/beber 14
dust baths/baños con
  tierra 16
eating/comer 12
eggs/huevos 4, 20

feathers/plumas 6, 16
hens/gallinas 8
insects/insectos 12, 16
pecking/picotear 10
predators/
  depredadores 18
roosters/gallos 8
scratching/escarbar 10
water/agua 14

About the Author/Información sobre la autora

JoAnn Early Macken is the author of two rhyming picture books, *Sing-Along Song* and *Cats on Judy*, and four other series of nonfiction books for beginning readers. Her poems have appeared in several children's magazines. A graduate of the M.F.A. in Writing for Children and Young Adults program at Vermont College, she lives in Wisconsin with her husband and their two sons. Visit her Web site at www.joannmacken.com.

JoAnn Early Macken es autora de dos libros infantiles ilustrados en verso, *Sing-Along Song* y *Cats on Judy*, y también de cuatro series de libros de corte realista dirigidos a los lectores principiantes. Sus poemas han sido publicados en varias revistas para niños. Graduada del M.F.A. en Redacción para niños y adultos jóvenes del Vermont College, vive en Wisconsin con su esposo y sus dos hijos. Visita su página Web. www.joannmacken.com.

Berwyn Public Library
2701 Harlem Ave.
Berwyn, IL 60402

3 2957 00259 9408